This book belongs to:

Nico Oliver
lots of love from
Great Aunty Fiona

Marvin's aunty Dora and mum Tui nesting.

Nadia was excited to capture the birth of Marvin on her phone.

Nadia feeding Marvin his favourite food, steamed mussels.

Minutes after Marvin was born.

Marvin slept in a box by the
fireplace for the first 8 weeks.

Big brother Bodhi's artwork
of Marvin and his egg.

Dad Rocky and Mum Tui meet little
Marvin for the first time.

Marvin, I like playing
with you

 Bodhi

For my big human brothers Bodhi and River, love Marvin (and Nadia)

For my sisters Morag and Shelagh, two good chooks! — Fifi

First published in 2020 by Scholastic New Zealand Limited
Private Bag 94407, Botany, Auckland 2163, New Zealand

Scholastic Australia Pty Limited
PO Box 579, Gosford, NSW 2250, Australia

Text © Nadia Lim, 2020
Illustrations © Fifi Colston, 2020

ISBN 978-1-77543-724-6

A catalogue record for this book is available from the National Library of New Zealand.

12 11 10 9 8 7 6 5 4 3 2 1   0 1 2 3 4 5 6 7 8 9 / 2

Illustrations created in pencil and digital media

Publishing team: Lynette Evans, Penny Scown and Abby Haverkamp
Designer: Smartwork Creative, www.smartworkcreative.co.nz
Typeset in Chaloops 21/36pt
Printed in New Zealand by Wickliffe NZ Limited

Scholastic New Zealand's policy is to use papers that are renewable and made efficiently from
wood grown in responsibly managed forests, so as to minimise its environmental footprint.

Nadia Lim's
Marvellous
MARVIN

Inspired by a TRUE STORY
Pictures by FIFI COLSTON

SCHOLASTIC
AUCKLAND SYDNEY NEW YORK LONDON TORONTO
MEXICO CITY NEW DELHI HONG KONG

The hens had laid some pretty eggs,
but if the truth be told,
they then forgot to sit on them ...

and those eggs are getting cold!

The eggs need to be rescued . . .
kind hands come swooping in.
And Mama puts them, warm and safe,
inside her best cake tin!

Mama counts them, 1 . . . 2 . . . 3 . . . 4 . . .

each one's a treasure chest.
But how many chicks will hatch?
Can you make a guess?

**CHEEP-CHEEP!
PECK-PECK!**

One day there is a crack,
and cheeping from the smallest egg,
the one way at the back.

First there comes an egg tooth,
then a yellow beak to see,
peck-pecking at the eggshell,
until that chick is free.

"My, oh my, you're MARVELLOUS!"
Mama whispers happily.

"Welcome Marvellous Marvin,
to our little family."

Marvin is a handsome boy,
bright-eyed, with a tickly tum.
A bundle of sooty feathers,

and a fluffy white bum!

CHEEP-CHEEP!
PECK-PECK!

Marvellous Marvin says
HELLO.
Then there is no stopping him,
that chick is on the go...

peeking in the mirror,

pecking at his food,

pulling up a worm or two

and playing peek-a-boo.

He hides among the seedlings,
his favourite is bok choy.
His Mama calls and calls and CALLS...

Marvin is an **ADVENTUROUS** boy.

Joining his brothers for breakfast,
Mama's pancakes are pure joy.
But watch that food upon your plate . . .

Marvin is a
HUNGRY boy.

Climbing on Dad's shoulder,
he isn't at all coy.

But then, SPLAT . . .

and OOPS . . .

and POOPS . . .

Marvin is a MESSY boy.

Snuggling up at bedtime,
with a hot-water bottle toy.
Marvin is safe and loved.

He is a MARVELLOUS boy.

Nadia's Egg-citing Farm Facts about Chickens

- Baby chickens are called chicks. Female/girl chickens are called pullets until they are old enough to lay eggs, and then they are called hens. Male/boy chickens are called cockerels until they start crowing, and then they are called roosters.

- You can't tell the gender of a chicken when it is born. You can only tell it's a male once it starts crowing and/or growing a comb on top of its head.

- In the wild, a rooster will often search out a perfect spot for one of the hens to nest. This nesting spot could be anywhere that he feels is a safe place to lay eggs. Two of the strangest nesting spots my hens have had is our gumboot rack and the outdoor fireplace!

- Chickens can recognise the faces of over 100 different people and animals.

- Without a rooster, a hen's eggs won't be fertilised, so won't develop into young chicks. A fertilised egg will only start developing if it is kept warm (at a perfect temperature of 37.5 °C) underneath a mother hen, or in an incubator, for 21 days. During this time, a mother hen will only leave her nest and eggs for no more than 20 minutes a day (just enough time to get some food and water and go to the toilet!).

There are more than 500 breeds of chickens throughout the world and they all look very different. Marvin's dad, Rocky, is a Barred Plymouth Rock, and his mum, Tui, is an Orpington.

Different breeds of chickens lay different coloured eggs. Most eggs are brown or white, however you can also get pale blue, olive green, nude pink and copper coloured eggs! The colour has nothing to do with their taste or nutrition — all are equally delicious and nutritious.

After incubating for 21 days, it can take up to 24 hours for a chick to escape the shell after it has made its first break in the internal membrane of the egg (called 'pipping'). Often it takes much less time, but around 24 hours is fairly common.

Chickens poo a lot, about 12-15 times a day, sometimes even more! And they even poo at night while they are sleeping. But did you know that, out of all animal poo, chicken poo is the highest in nitrogen, an important element that soil needs to help plants grow. We put the chicken poo in our compost and use it to fertilise our gardens for great veggies!

Mother hens talk to their chicks while they're still inside the eggs, and the chicks can chirp back while in the shell. I remember hearing Marvin chirping from inside his shell the day before he hatched!

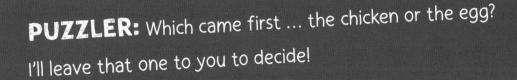

PUZZLER: Which came first … the chicken or the egg? I'll leave that one to you to decide!

Nadia's Egg-cellent Fluffy Saturday Pancakes Recipe

I'm willing to bet these are THE lightest, fluffiest pancakes you will have ever eaten. Ever. It's all thanks to beating the eggs and folding them through the batter, keeping them super light and fluffy. Use gluten-free flour to make them gluten-free.

Serves 4 | Preparation time: 10 minutes | Cook time: 15 minutes

Ingredients

2 **eggs**

2 tablespoons **sugar**

1 ½ cups **self-raising flour** (or plain flour with 1 ½ teaspoons baking powder added)

1 teaspoon **baking powder**

¾ cup **milk** (soy, oat or cow's)

Finely grated zest of 1 **lemon** or orange (optional)

1 punnet fresh **blueberries** (or ¾ cup frozen blueberries, defrosted and drained)

Oil for cooking (I use coconut oil)

Method

1 Place eggs and sugar in a large mixing bowl. Use an electric eggbeater to beat eggs and sugar until very light, pale and fluffy.

2 Sift in flour and baking powder.

3 Add milk and zest (if using) and use a large metal spoon to gently fold the batter together, keeping it as light and airy as possible. Add a little more milk if needed.

4 Gently stir in blueberries.

5 Heat a teaspoon of oil in a large non-stick frypan over medium heat. Cook pancakes (about 2 tablespoons of mixture per pancake) for 2–3 minutes on one side until bubbles appear on the surface. Then flip delicately with a spatula or fish slice to cook for a further 2 minutes or so on other side or until puffed and golden.

You should be able to cook 3–4 pancakes at a time. Cook in batches, adding more oil as needed. When cooked, remove to a plate and cover with tinfoil to keep warm.

6 Serve with sliced banana or strawberries, yoghurt and a little drizzle of maple syrup.

 Eat and enjoy!

Marvin loves to help harvest vegetables from the glasshouse and garden.

Marvin eagerly waiting for Saturday pancakes.

Bodhi loves the eggs that Marvin's mum and aunties lay every day.

Marvin and brother River love playing in the sandpit.

Marvin loves hanging out on Carlos's shoulder, but Carlos isn't so sure!

Marvin helping River to feed a lamb.

A Word about Marvin

Hello! I hope you have enjoyed reading about Marvellous Marvin's cheeky endeavours.

Marvin's story is real – he is my chick that I ended up hatching in the middle of winter 2020. We have freezing winters in Arrowtown, where I live, and I knew the chicks wouldn't survive in the nest, so I took the four eggs and placed them in one of my cake tins, surrounded by lots of cosy straw. Then I placed the tin on a big stack of books with a lamp over the top to keep the eggs nice and warm. Only one chick hatched – you know his name!

From birth he was a real cool chick, never leaving my side. He grew up inside our house for the first eight weeks of his life, sleeping in a cardboard box with straw and a hot-water bottle. He now lives outside in his own chicken coop house that is just outside my kitchen window, so I see him every morning. He is super friendly and loves perching on my shoulder and being stroked. He is still very cheeky and tries to sneak back into the house every now and again … and will steal food off your plate if you're not looking! He even pulls up my plants in the garden!

Thanks to you for helping the charities **HUHA** (Helping You Help Animals), who rescue and re-home lots of animals, and **Garden to Table**, who run programmes in primary schools teaching kids how to grow, harvest and cook their own food. All of Marvin's and my author profits go directly to these two wonderful charities.

Thank you so much to Lynette Evans and the Scholastic team for bringing Marvin's story to life.

Bye for now! (*Cheep cheep!* says Marvin.)

Nadia and Marvin xx

This little birdie tells me there are more **Marvellous Marvin** farm adventures coming, don't miss out!

CHEEP-CHEEP!